OneOnOne

Jack Myers

[handwritten inscription: For Bruce, in admiration for your work, Jack]

OneOnOne

poems

Autumn House Press PITTSBURGH

OneOnOne: Poems

ISBN 0-9669419-0-X
Library of Congress Catalog Card Number: 98-74999

Cover and text design: Kathy Boykowycz
Printed in the United States of America

Published by Autumn House Press, a not-for-profit publisher specializing in poetry and other fine literature.

Autumn House Press
219 Bigham Street
Pittsburgh, Pennsylvania 15211

Acknowledgements

Some of the poems that appear in this volume have been previously published in the following journals and books: *American Literary Review, The American Poetry Review, The American Scholar, The Aurora, Chicago Review, Columbia Poetry Review, Dominion Review, Defined Providence, The Eleventh Muse, The Harvard Advocate, The Nebraska Review, The Onset Review, The Pittsburgh Quarterly* (on-line), *Poetry* (Chicago), *Poetry East, The Southern Review, Southern Florida Review, Southwest Review, Sycamore Review, Third Coast, Willow Springs*

"Bread, Meat, Greens, and Soap" and "The Stripper" were first published in *Poetry* and copyrighted © by The Modern Poetry Association, June 1993. "It's Not my Cup of Tea" was first published in *Poetry*, and copyrighted © in 1996. "Doing and Being: A Story About the Buddha," "Going Up, Coming Down," and "The Optimist, The Pessimist, and the Other" were published and copyrighted © by The Modern Language Association in May 1997 (Double Anniversary Issue).

"Agoraphobic" appeared in *Outsiders* (Milkweed Books, 1999).

"Bread, Meat, Greens, and Soap," "Taking the Children Away," "Narcissus," "It's Not my Cup of Tea," and "True West" also appeared in *Leaning House Poets*, a CD/anthology from Leaning House Jazz Records, Dallas, 1996

"Admitting the Dark" was also published in *Best Texas Writing*, Rancho Loco Press, 1997; "On Introspection" in *Best Texas Writing 1998*, Fire Wheel Press.

"Limits" was published by Poetry in Motion for the Dallas Area Rapid Transit System, 1999.

Some of these poems were published as a chapbook: *Human Being*, Rancho Loco Press, Dallas, 1998.

I would like to thank Southern Methodist University for the generosity of a Special Research Fellowship Leave that played a strong supporting role in helping to bring the present work to fruition.

And last but not least, I want to thank Ralph Angel, Mark Cox, Tony Hoagland, Michael Simms, and Thea Temple for their perceptive and painstaking editorial work on this manuscript.

• Jack Myers

The publisher would like to thank Jerry Costanzo, Sam Hazo, and Ed Ochester for their wise counsel. And a special thanks to Frank Lehner.

• Michael Simms

Contents

Once when the family took a trip
and stopped
> *at a motel*
you cried and cried.
We thought that you were ill.
Then at last you said
"Why did
> *we have*
>> *to move*
to this small house?"

> • John Logan, *"Poem for my Son"*

for Thea Temple
and for all those not in their places

and for Patricia Dussair, Gatekeeper

Attention

At first as a child
I collected words,
slurring them together
into a single blur,
until I thought what I felt.

Then I collected others' words,
words so wise and irreducible
I thought they taught me how to grasp.

They felt like a kind of immortality
but they only insured
I could never use them
whenever I inquired after myself.

Now what's left is the rest of my life
and what looked like a sail
is just the billowing of a shirt.

And I don't know what I want or feel
beyond a long inhale on something
that makes me feel like I'm sailing.

Because once you get into being scared
it's endlessly divisible. Soon
we'll all be wearing masks
like explanations during sex.

Then there's this feeling I have
on the border of simple being
not even the sleep of words can reach.

I can feel it like my first-grade handwriting
under all the philosophy I think. And it's not
the thought of that child that's stopped
time, it's how he got stuck in his sleep.

All I can figure is it must've been
something I missed when I wasn't paying attention,
when I was waiting for revelation,

collecting smoke and sparks from my departures
and concluding with every departure
only another departure will do.

Admitting the Dark

Everything that has been said...
is hurled through high windows
into a big hole my father calls heaven *but I call* the sky

• *John Engman, "Atlantis"*

The old Jewish men of my town
with their breath stinking of fish tins
and nasty dispositions, and debts,
and abstinence from everything
ever called lovely had it right.

Even as a child they seemed short to me
in their baggy suits and songs droning
like locust swarming the desert, their dance,
a rock trying to free itself from running away.

I'd slip by their moaning synagogue at dusk
as if it were the lair of larvae, pass quietly
by my fright thinking I had escaped the day
they finally pulled me in and stuck me
in my place and made me kiss the black
Book of the Dead that praised the Glory of God
in such saturating colors it made no sense.

Now all those who sang for the dead
are dead. And the boys who ran away,
emptied the town of marriages and shops
and abandoned it to commuters, have laid pain
to sleep, and sleep in a life that walls out death
and so made death surround them.

What strength it took to feel so weak, to rock
in place and sing of death. Of course it was dark.
That's what they sang about. Even my heart,
surrounded by darkness like way back then,
which is always beating faster in spite of me, knows that.

True West

The knowledge of all that he betrayed
Grew till it was the same whether he stayed
Or went. Therefore he went.

• W.S. Merwin, "Odysseus"

I'm obsessed with driving out west
though I live in the West.
I mean farther, inward,
one hard right turn
past the squintings of cactus
and the shadows of birds
who live off the dead
and doze on a column of wind.

I'll feel larger inside
there at the canyon's edge
though I know this world's no more
than the tip of a nib on a piece of felt
the immortal gods shoot pool on.

I can no more prove I have a soul
than I can take an armful of silence
as it's evaporating
and bring it back as proof.

Mother never got there
though she felt close
dancing by herself
to Frank Sinatra.
Father just got littler
and more distant
screaming at everyone
keep away.

I can feel it building in me
the way silence around ruins
grows more sacred
and mysterious over time.

Someone once lived here
I'll say when I get there,
walking around sweating
in the rock and heat
and awe of it,
trying to imagine who.

Agoraphobic

Here in my little place,
making poems, making sleep,
a glass of water so clear
it hurts, I have learned acceptance
from the rain that wipes out its losses
with new losses, how like the epiphany
of an after-image it suddenly struck me
everything I bought this year happened to be blue.

Even the little *tsk* on the dial of my electric blanket
set to preserve me in sleep offers peace,
and the telephone holding back and bulging
and holding back harder before it explodes
has kept my childish wanting-to-be-wanted in check.

Yesterday I sprinkled some rosemary,
which stands for remembrance and fidelity,
into my virgin olive oil. I thought, like it,
if I can wait the winter out inside
as it slowly turns green, when I open it,
it'll be my wild spring in Greece.

Once in a while I eat just enough to burst forth
and lay claim to something calling me out there.
It happened with a shirt I bought
that already seemed so much a part of me,
it exposed my deepest fear.
It had so many pockets and pleats
that the thought of ironing it
practically exhausted me, and before I knew it

I was engulfed in another relationship
so complex and delicate that upon leaving,
I stood outside my door,
my back to the world,
like an announcement —
I could not, for the life of me,
turn around — Blunderer, Oaf,
the sum total of me overwhelmed
once more on the edge of being noticed.

The Initiate

Like Zeno, I tried to break down the mechanics of motion
to capture the essence of movement minus the motion,
practiced how to close my eyes and then open them,
one position after another, until I learned the entire series by rote.

I tried and re-tried in order to pass through trying,
noting others, like avatars, who were only mothers,
effortlessly flood whatever they did with light.

I was at my best when I was spontaneous and unconscious,
a paradox who, blessed when he didn't know he was blessed,
yearned to be holy so he could turn and bless himself.

Odd to spend one's life learning how to close one's eyes
then open them. Well, at least there was that, and it was good.
And I thought it might help with something else.

Doing and Being:
A Story About the Buddha

For a hundred thousand eons, or *kalpas*,
before his birth, the Buddha practiced
patience and compassion, steadfastness and calm.

Each *kalpa* was one hundred thousand years long,
yet the Buddha secretly smiled, sitting at his practice
which was said to be twice the size of Mt. Everest.

It is said his progress was like that of the raven
who once every hundred years appeared
with a silk scarf in its beak
which it dragged lightly over the mountain top
and thus gradually wore the mountain down.

It was in this way that the Buddha became Buddha.

It's Not My Cup of Tea

My wife wants to know
what difference does it make
what cup I drink from,
and I complain
I like what I like
and that's the story.

We have many kinds of cups.
But this morning my favorite is dirty
and I'm hunting for something
that won't make me think:

One's a fertility goddess,
huge fructuous belly, little head.

Another's pleasant enough for guests,
but has to have its finicky little saucer
underneath so it won't feel embarrassed.

And another, which is a smaller version
of what I like, would require me
to get up and down too many times.

You think I am spoiled
or too set in my ways
or that I'm difficult
to live with,
and you're right.

But there are so few things
that fit me in this life
I can count them on one hand,
things the spirit can sleep in
because whoever made them
put the things of this world —
vanity, greed, a sentimental wish
to be small again — aside.

I know, I could've found my cup
and washed it
and then I'd have my cup.
But it's not my cup I want.

Passing Through

Energy in a closed system,
though it may be transformed,
is constant.
Matter cannot be created or destroyed.

• *Mulligan*, Practical Physics

Each night as I bore through the blurry presences
of trees bending over this dip in the road,
I hollow out a tunnel to a word
behind the word not said.

It whispers if you shut off the lights
and let the darkness softly light the night
and melt your body, you will pass right through
whoever's coming at you.

I can feel the dew's resistance to surrendering
into being drawn up molecule by molecule
into the fireball whispering "You can do it!"

And just as I was about to prove
that faith has an effect on energy,
I find I'm taking credit for what I am,
cheapening what is holy into the trick
of turning wine back into water.

Was Akhenaton, in his heart of hearts, like me,
or did the glory of his radiant humility help
lift the sun by just that much?

self to Self

*..even the enlightened person remains what he is,
and is never more than his own limited ego before
the One who dwells within him...."*

• *Carl Jung,* Antwort auf Hiob

I empty myself of self
and dive down in.

The rain falling
has risen from the lake
that's rising from the rain.

I have eyes I cannot close.
One right fin.

I steer in circles
and the circles stir me.

Soon I will be the color of water
harvested from air, thickened by distance.

I do not know which of us is seeping in
but I am closing the distance
by drinking it in.

Either I will finally become who I am,
or, swallowing the distance between us,
soon I will loom as large as him.

Away

The boy's been punished again
and pushed to his room.
He sits there all ears,
listening to his disappearance
so hard he can feel
the bacterial silence
colonize the waiting,
then the waiting grow huge,
blot out like a suicidal impulse
that makes the waiting last
as long as he lives.

Mother's flying around the kitchen
downstairs like a Chagall dark angel,
thunderous pots over a tiny atoll.
Father is a ship sailing by,
a metal smile wincing on the horizon.

The boy swallows it all,
especially the pure blue distance
that teaches each new moment it is
obsolete, then erases the last.

He erases the past and runs away
again and again until at last
like those wagon wheels
in Western movies
that spin so fast
they change directions
without stopping,
his leaving feels like
an arrival.

It's amazing how something trivial
turns out to be the story of your life,
like how I held up
different colored Jujubes
to the light of a spectacular
Technicolor emptiness
and loved chewing on their guts,
how something so much itself,
that intrigued and nonplused him,
changed everything into itself.

Club Fighters

When mother lost it
and turned inside-out
with anger, she'd hit me
with whatever came to hand,
her hand, a broom, a brush,
whatever domestic weapon
an unhappy housewife used
to clean things up
around the house.

But I was a survivor too.
I could add things up, roll
all those terrifying, mantric blows
into one death-defying punch,
then figure, proudly, if this were
real life then I'd be dead.

I said let me do it for you, mother,
I'm good at this. Watch how
I don't blink. This is how
a boxer trains, staring down
barrages in a corner,
welcoming punishment
into his body
like nourishment
while he goes somewhere else.

I felt like a punch drunk fighter
who never throws a punch,
a journeyman who, night after night,
guts it out while everyone
in the house screams like a mob
of angry mothers, "Do something!"
meaning, do something else.

Well, I'm doing it for you, mother,
I'm beating myself up, putting in
my solo, unconscious appearance
to honor your unhappiness
with me and everything else.
Maybe I'll be cleaning the house
when it begins, but it begins
with a feeling that's immense,
then ends gradually and vaguely
and badly, with me standing there
in the absence of ruins,
feeling I am someone else.

The Glowing River

The spin I'd put on my father's wanting to be alone
would be to compare him to the solitary males of the wild kingdom
whose nobility and courage disdained the flock, the herd,
the whole squawking barbecue of fear and indecision.

But when I look his isolation in the eye I see
he couldn't love easily, though he felt so deeply
he spent all his life resisting it,

like the nuclear power plant that recycled so much warm water
it choked its lake on weeds, so they stocked it with weed-eating fish
who, in my mind, prospered so well that I knew soon something
larger, more ominous and foreign would arrive.

They would gather at the mouth of the underwater river
and, basking in the heat of its eerie, greenish glow,
fall asleep under the spell of an alien sun.

You see the problem, how the unnatural, over time, spawns something
stranger than we'd meant. Which is why I'm studying my nature through
what must've happened to my father. Toxic secrets beyond the mouth
of the glowing river I'll never learn but like all sons have put my faith in.

Keepers of the Past

*Everywhere there's a dead end
there's an opening.*

• *Thea Temple*

I can hear the roaring of the Minotaur.
But I want to see it. My father fears me
gored to death. I tell him if we could see
what we fear then we could reason with it.

He says though he built the maze himself
he can't find his own way out, then looks up
and says idealistically, "But the sky is free."
Nonsense. He thinks his fear will save me.

I can see him figuring me out
the way he made me a necklace
by tying a thread to an ant
that spiraled through empty shells.

But I was a child and believed him when he said
he captured the sound of the sea for me.

My plan is to grab the Minotaur
by the balls and squeeze
until it's unconscious,
then roll it over the cliff.

We stand here deciding
how to thread history through fate
like two of the Immortals.
But we are only a father and son deciding
a lifetime, it seems.

Inviolate

For months I was stuck inside the sound
of things breaking: stone foundations cracking,
steel snapping, and whatever I did continued
that split-second clap of the sound of things collapsing.

I asked Daedalus, keeper of the bulging past,
to sleep with Beauty, for I knew while she would make
a maze of her surrender against his force of will
I'd have time to trap what I was feeling and pour

a circle of gas around their tryst and light it
with my blinding sleep. Yes, sleep in the burning
palm of my unconsciousness and be done to a crisp.

But you know how time in fairy tales takes time
to change things into something purer than we'd meant:
My heroes made a separate bargain:
she was to sink more deeply into what I might
become if I lived long enough, while he would lay
the way with mazes from the life unlived before me.

In Bagdabastan This is a Fruit

In Bagdabastan this is a fruit.

>*It looks strange.*
>*We don't want it.*

It eases stubbornness with its stubbornness
because it has absorbed the lesson of the rain
that softened our rugged landscape into grains of sand.

>*We have no fruit here.*
>*We do not want this fruit.*

Inside it has many luscious seeds.
In truth, it is made entirely of seeds
packed together, yet each seed is kept
separate, wrapped as if for a long journey.

>*There are no long journeys here.*
>*We do not need this fruit.*

That is why I offer you this fruit.
Where we live we already have it.
In fact, we cultivate it with great care
though it would do just as well without us.

>*We don't want this fruit.*
>*We will do without it.*

If I may say so, that is now impossible
since it is already something you so greatly oppose.
If I take it away you will never be rid of it.

>*For the last time, we do not want this fruit.*
>*It is not something we require.*

Fine, then I will leave it here with you,
for we have found it is something we cannot do without.
If you accept it, you won't know how you've done without it.
Then you'll be able to do without it.

Narcissus

I am still hypnotized by perfection,
still hostage to a glimpse:
the curve of that woman's leg,
some distant musical laughter,
fierce micro-bursts of intimacy

that desolate the evening,
leave tomorrow stuck on flashback
and all the sweat and songs of years
stunned and obliterated
by a dazzling cameo appearance.

I should write tiny poems
on the wind about wine and love
like the great minimal poet Rumi
who invented the Whirling Dervishes
and spiraled into climax
and got stuck inside the glimpse.

I want to know who I was as a child,
how I came to be left paralyzed
and fevered like a tree by its greenery,
dreaming and swaying and futilely reaching out
while mad birds hop and screech inside it.

What comfort to be plain and blind
and smug inside the given,
to be swallowed whole and live
in a house of dead wood
and delivered from desire.

What terror to be beautiful and immobile,
kissed against a taut blue skin of water
while something out of nowhere,
something broken off within me,
outside memory or purpose,
plummets murderously down.

The Second Hunger

What was I looking at
when I kissed your mouth
and held myself there
like a lion
engorged on a mirage?

What was I holding
when you sank against me
and held me there
the way a dream holds its sleeper?

There's nothing to be afraid of
I said. But today we look ugly,
walk all which-ways in wrinkled clothes
that look like opposing banners
shredded in battle.

This is not to berate you
for giving yourself to me —
I, too, "desired my dust
to be mingled with yours
forever and forever and forever" —
it is for what hunger
can do to us. I who am sick
of my needs, then, blink,
am hungry again.

If that was love,
if that was lust,
it's nothing to fool around with.

Now the ceremony of emptiness
that slammed us together
will make whichever one of us
is still left standing
when it's over
say it's over.

There's nothing to be afraid of,
I said. Even now
as I hold your face
and feel my hands
have been blown off,
and kiss your mouth
as if I'm calling for help
with no mouth, I tell you
there's nothing to be afraid of.

Mr. Muscle Beach and the
Aerobics Instructor

have left each other. They believed deeply
in their Spartan diet, the satori-like clang
of their weights, in teasing each other
like the miniature shaggy dog they co-owned
running obsessively back and forth between them.

I loved being amazed at their bodies,
the sheen of their flawless skin,
as if sheer belief in working out
and the exhilaration of exhaustion
had sculpted minarets out of their bodies.

But tonight I found them all moved out.
The ascetic intensity of right devotional thinking
had swept through their apartment, leaving behind
only a set of weights in the corner, and the puppy,
who wouldn't come out, trembling under them.

Last

They are wise to send their strongest first, I thought.
And I kissed her.

        • *Robert Creeley, "A Form of Adaption"*

I think I am too little to love.
There's just a nickel of me left,
enough to hold on to, a child's allowance
that feels so big, so real, I bite into it
and it tastes bitter and metallic
like a difficult decision.

What is something certain and nearly
worthless against your dusky grace,
eyes that glittered and burned through
my blackout. That emerald sea you took me to

was just a big distraction, a commotion
of costume jewelry. Leashed to my needs,
I marched back and forth across the sugary sand —
yes, no, yes, about-face, foolish man — as if after
my suicide I could decide how to prepare my death.

Am I living deeply enough in the moment for you?

I am too tired to prepare a new way to my ruin
though my history shows I could borrow against
whatever I'd be without you to make the way beautiful.

You're so lovely you could have ten of me.
You can afford to be careless. I'm not that special.
Terrified, I held my breath as you bowed over me
and lifted my face like a delicately exhausted,
wing-seeded dandelion.

I have always overcome my losses by becoming larger
by being dispersed. I feel so close to nothing now
if I ever let go and you left me, as you will surely do,
I would be complete, the ancient cycle of longing
left longing to complete itself.

Taking the Children Away

They will pack the sky blue car
with blankets and pillows
and puzzles and snacks,
enough to end a life,
and the last thing I will see
will be the stuffed animals
pressed against the window,
like a happy ending in a Muppet movie,
tiny hands like wings
waving goodbye, little voices
trailing out the sides like streamers.

I will stand there
in the suicidal, accelerating, horizontal draft
of the car longer than is natural,
feeling liberated,
like a bombed-out town,
as the sad blue car dwindles and darkens
and inhales itself,
and I enter the house,
turn off the lights,
sit in foreclosure,
watching the twinkling half-life
of fallout begin floating down the years,
scattered toys appearing one by one
the way the first evening stars
look left behind.

This must be the missing that begins
inside the waiting for something larger
to take over, the being over to be over
that feels like the cobalt hand of air
I think my soul must be. I am afraid
that it will take a breath and then another
and another, like steps, until I begin to glow
like the small dull bulb inside a doorbell
as the evening sun slowly, simply disappears.

Blue Bayou Rooms

*What is desire but the wish for some
relief from the self....*

• *Stephen Dobyns*

5 a.m. and the glowing aqua pool
pours through itself restlessly,
flowers sexually like the glide of a saxophone
washing over and through the black railings
of the balconies, passes whole through the sliding
glass doors, and freshens the oxidized walls of my bedroom
where I wake to a sky-blue blush
whose implosive slow-motion climax
rolls the bodies of sleepers over in an undertow.

This could be a beautiful place
if it were not for the abortion
that brought young Yolanda here,
whose black skin glistens in the sun
like a dazzled shadow as she glides
underwater the length of the pool.

This could be a beautiful place
if Leo, fresh from the barbarities
of biopsies at the V.A. hospital,
would come out of his room and forget
his wife of 50 years, buried with lymphoma.
The sound of people idling in their rooms,
forlornly smoking and drinking from memory,
then sleeping while the fear-ridden cockroaches,
alert as lasers, skitter on their humorless rounds,
is like the monotonous moan of the exhausted
diesel bus that waits to take us to work.

Desire's lover is sadness and she's in his skin,
having surrendered her lilac silks with a sigh
that splashes orchestrally against the windows
and swells through memory as fresh blood to a bruise.

I would like all the people to come out on their balconies.
There'd be music and laughter and flowers like in New Orleans,
The Big Easy, and for the women we'd pour vegetables and shadows,
the fruit of our hearts, *legumbres, penumbres, naranjas,*
until this lost place that will not heal remembers that the sadness
that brought us here we made for each other as tenderly and sparely
as a lonely meal.

All the blinds are closed,
but we know the pool is out there
in the dark, shining like a tourmaline,
the way we've forgotten the first shy girl
we fell in love with, but feel the way her smile
sunk in and said no, that the water is gorgeous
just because of a thin blue slap of paint.
No one lives here, not really.
No one ever comes out.
Day, like the pool, turns sickly
in daylight, and lifting the cover
off the filters, roaches and black leaves swirl
like the nightmare in which we are singled out and drowned.

We are all afraid of the pool.

The Buddha on Synchronicity

In another life, the Buddha set out to dig a well.
Naming each basket of dirt for one of his failings,
he spread anger on top of impatience and impatience on top of lust
and threw the lime of mistrust in for good measure.

When he was chest-deep and exhausted from exhuming
himself through his faults, he stood knee-deep in muck.
Where others had said, "I have tried to build a well and found
only mud," the Buddha cried, "Good, I have found water!"

And having dug long enough and deep, with the leftover dirt
he made a foundation, with the leftover mud he made bricks. Thus
by digging down to clear water, he was ready to build his house.

Bread, Meat, Greens, and Soap

It feels like deja vu all over again.

• *Yogi Berra*

I feel like I'm about to be fired,
or my doctor will say I have
the obstruction he suspected,
or my 2nd-story-divorce-efficiency apartment
will be rubbed out by a clear blue sky
when I get back.

For instance, right now I'm walking around
this brand new cost-saver supermarket
conscious of this weird impingement
of loss, the way amputees feel the ache
of a phantom limb only I'm talking about all of me,
when I stop and ask an illegal alien stockboy
what street is this, and he croons to me
"Larmanda, Larmanda," which means Larmanda,
some nameless City Father's long lost wife,
and I realize, Holy Mackerel, right where I'm standing,
between the fresh fish and the meatcase
is my old bedroom where me and Willa,
which means Willa, made love everyday
after laps and breaststrokes in the pool
of our lovely torn-down walk-up.
And not fifty feet away, years ago,
behind the pharmacy, I slipped a disc
but kept on crawling forward, thinking
who on earth has stabbed me in the back?

Right here in the hyped-up screaming
of the cereal aisle, the kids used to fly around
the kitchen like cartoon characters.
I wanted to grab the old lady
blocking my bedroom with her cart
and argue about this, let her know
how it was with us, but then I figured
what's the use, what are you going to do
about a past that is now
hundreds of thousands of tons of processed food,
a seven-billion-pound carrot to keep me going?

See how crazy with excitement I can get,
as if my life were living proof
of the Unified Field Theory,
which, in fact, to anyone who's hungry
is business as usual, a big so what?
Like taking pride in a miserable grocery list.
I mean, if you can feel it
about to rain in your bones,
and goddamn monkeys and geese
can sense a disaster
a priori,
if someone with some cash
can raze the past
and plunk a Safeway down on top of it,
then what else needs to happen before
the future will have me convinced?

I consult my list, the instructions I wrote
that amount to a soap opera on how to keep going,
written with such a magnificent sense of ease,
such amputated detachment, that right here in the store
I'm firing myself, divorcing the past from the present,
saying, Get your things,
just get what you came to get
and get out.

A Finger Pointing at the Moon
is Not the Moon Itself

...it is like the Noh: whenever the script says
dances, *whatever the actor does next is a dance. If he*
stands still, he is dancing.

• *Jack Gilbert, "To See If Something Comes Next"*

When the mystics went into the desert
to break off a little wisdom
or climbed mountains and sat in caves
to feel whole and empty
or looked at the entrails of animals
to see what would happen
or vision-quested for their spirit animal
to see who they were
or dreamed into the face of rocks
to see what they felt
or spun into a blur
to erase what they felt
or refused to eat
to stop thinking
or ate gorgeous toxins
to think vividly
or died and came back
to see if they could,

when they came back to us,
having balanced the extremes
in themselves with the extraordinary,
speaking in gibberish and parables
about what it is to be us,
we couldn't understand them.
Basically, we thought they said
"It's all right to be us, keep trying,"
and, looking down, we shook our heads
the way gods do at mortals,
for we were already ourselves, weren't we? —
and we went on with our lives.

Desiring Not Desiring

Sitting on the edge, flickering between living
in the tumultuous night-sparkling cities of desire
and the pure blue air of not-desiring flooding in
behind his meditation on breathing,

the Buddha's body shrank like a rotting apple
and his soul sweat the air with sweetness.
He did not ask "What do I *want*?"
in the same way, as a child, I demanded to know
"When will I grow up?"

You see the problem....

On Thinking About Introspection

A man is flying with a mirror
for a headlight, flying headfirst
into a mirror. The man in the mirror

looks still. It is the way that is
flying backward, he thinks, pouring

like slag into the still blue sky.
He feels he has no face, is blind
as a mirror with the face of a man

looking at his face. The way feels huge,
blocked: mother, father, sister, brother,
others streaming out of the crowded mirror

holding mirrors, circling back, flying along
with him. This armada is reassuring, he thinks,
and so he feels he can speak for the others.

But the mirror feels the same. I don't need
this man, the mirror thinks just as the man
thinks the same thing. Neither one knows he thinks

the same thing though each one can tell
what the other is thinking but not which one
is thinking it, nor how all of this began.

The River of Karma

Midnight. A white moth holds fast
to its reflection on the steel molding
of the men's room floor.

It must've seen the light of the room
as a square moon
and miraculously flown through it.

Checking on him all week
between wanting this and not wanting that,
I think, like him, I am more important.

If I threw him out into the night
he might die a better death
or live a little longer
but without him
as my little forget-me-not
I'd forget the problem with desire.

Why Couldn't He Stop?

The temple bell stops.
But the sound keeps coming
Out of the flowers.

> • *Basho*

Francesca says, "Your clavicles, how beautiful!"
But I like the place where her thighs flow into hips
for which there is no name except the rolling
intonation of depth after a Li Po poem.

He folded thousands of poems
into little paper boats
and floated them downriver.
Lived alone, drank a lot,
and lives like that forever.

Antoinette has a chipmunk's face, little nut-piercing teeth.
She knows she looks her best about ten feet off and so,
clever girl, has become a Marketing/Communications Specialist.

Francesca is Antigone. Her climaxes scare me. I have to cover her
mouth to contain the furies. Wouldn't it be nice, I used to think,
to have someone beautiful and deep, a cover-girl who's suffered?

When I told them of the time I fell overboard asleep, tied to
a speed boat heading toward Europe, how that's my life,
Francesca laughed and Antoinette's eyes turned two bright zeroes.

Why can't I just pick myself up
by my chopsticks
and forget about all this?

My beautiful daughter, who's possessed by twirling and laughing
and falling down, says, "What's this and this and this?" as she
touches the moles on my face. She senses there's been a mistake.

I say "They're only beauty marks, my little darling. God overdid."
Then she studies them, makes a face like she's taking medicine,
and then thinks, Forget about all this, as she twirls away asking
"Why couldn't He stop?"

On the Need to be Loved

I y'am what I y'am what I y'am.

• *Popeye*

My little daughter flops on top of me
as if I were a couch made out of a sunny day.

My youngest son thinks I am heroic,
even with my hands cut off at my pockets,
we walk off aimlessly to balance the day,
like twins.

My second son has grown a beard like mine
to oppose me, struggles hard to vanquish me
with difficult ideas.

My eldest son thinks I am a rock of wind,
a monument of absence he chisels into
with his cello.

And on certain days I can feel my ex-wives
vacuuming with the most articulated attachments
an emptiness only the will-to-forget can fill.

Which is why I was chimerical in their presence:
a couch, a hero, a rock of wind, until like steam
burst from both ends of my birth and death I rose up
from my life and, envying what I was, but wasn't,
I envied what I wasn't, but always was.

The Jewel's Jewel

The jewel hidden inside the rock
does not know it's a "jewel."

That name is hidden inside
a man in charge
of gargantuan machines.

Only when it's split open
and polished and sold and resold

so its worth soars as fabulously
as its vainglorious light

does the memory of the rock
it was hidden inside
become the jewel's jewel.

On Glimpsing Failure and Success

In a moment the Master transformed
his student's poem into a work
of great depth and resonance.

Then he said, "Sometimes I am skillful,
other days I cannot think of the word
for help. Today, we were lucky."

The student glimpsed the richness
of possibility, possibly fame before her.
Someday, she thought, she could be his equal.

The Master glimpsed how beautiful his student was,
sitting arched on her toes, just so, while intent on learning,
and how the moment, which he also noticed, flew past art.

Catching the Bird of Paradise

A weary old king, who had everything,
wanted to catch the fabulous bird of paradise.
In order to trap it, the king poured greed into beauty
and beauty back into greed and set the delicious elixir out
knowing only the *hausa*, the fabled bird of paradise
who flies on sunlit wings of freedom and detachment,
could drink from the potion and leave greed behind.

All day birds took turns alighting on the lip of the bowl,
which in itself was beautiful, but in the end the king grew angry
with the birds, for he could not tell if the *hausa* came or not
since he himself could not discern what was left behind.

The Stripper

Like fish surfacing from the long limousine
of streaming underwater currents, late afternoon
she appears at the pool mysteriously, flashing
the free-spending sun off men who turn helplessly
iridescent before her nakedness.

I have watched her discreetly, all summer long, carefully,
past what I take to be the usual shock and excitement
over closing in so quickly on what takes me so long to imagine.
Then scrupulously, clinically, I wait for what feels like
something minute and impossibly toxic to crystallize between us.

It'll take five years before her body softens and ripens
into the normalcy of the Kansas stock she comes from,
lying there legs splayed, contemptuous and bored with her
lavishly adored body which I imagine has nightly pumped dry
the grunts of anonymous drunks on the rank mud flats of desire.

She has no idea how tender, attentive, and appreciative
I could be, what an accident of luck it is to have such a body,
which she oils with unguents so slowly and luxuriously that I feel
luck rise through me all the way up here. Today it feels like we've been
married for years, that I've ended up bankrupt by her demands on me.
So I've become cruel, turning her body over and over in my mind,
coolly grading my stunning lascivious jewel by its imperfections.

Each day after nap time I come down and execute my perilous pass,
the formal, balding older gentleman from apartment 2B, who exchanges
dismissive looks with her. Today she has no idea I've decided to risk
everything I've fantasized (then step to her aid at the last minute)
as I march by shadowing her daydream with a complexly fashioned
"Pardon me" on my way to lodge an anonymous complaint with the manager.

Temperance

It must have been when Masamune
was doubled over his furnace,
looking into the fiery face
of his Emperor's command,
that he fantasized the languorous body
of his lover, the king's courtesan, Okoni,
and hammered and folded
and re-hammered and doubled over
the futility of his heart's desire
into 30,000 layers of molten steel
that took on the suppleness of lovers
crushed in the sheen of shot silk.

It must have been when he quenched
in cold water the hardness of bearing up
under never being other than what he was
that Masamune dutifully fashioned
an instrument to slash open the human body
in the prescribed classical ways
of those such as Okoni who betrayed
the Emperor, who, well pleased
with Masamune's work,
bestowed upon his servant the title,
Living Cultural Treasure.

Anima

The series of pictures culminates in the tenth when the hero, now perfectly at peace, walks unnoticed through the village streets. There is nothing extraordinary about him now except that all the trees burst into blossom as he passes by.

> • *Robert Johnson on Zen Buddhism's "Ten Oxherding Pictures"* (He: Understanding Masculine Psychology)

I was an expert
at throwing myself,
great arcing distances
at beautiful women.

When I awoke,
hugging them
as if I had found myself,
they were real
but I had no idea
who they were.

Then the flying glass,
the piercing arguments
in which we could not
see behind our needs.

I was a fish
who had heard
about the miraculous
thing called water
and swam off to find it
through nights sewn together
with rain, my mouth wide open
in a call.

Galatea, wise anima,
powerful sweet scent
of pressed almond,
electric blue aura,
I have grown twice
your age while you have waited
like Patience herself,
who has no sense of waiting,
for me to look at you again.

Mastery

At first we fought nobly against
what we could not do, but ended up
fighting against whatever prevented us
from getting what we want.

It is like the artist turned collector of art
who stops struggling against what he could not do
to become the master of what couldn't be done.

The Sound of One Hand Clapping

A young monk, distracted from meditation
by lustful imaginings, was told to observe
a corpse decay day after day for a month.

Bluish pallor, sunken skin, rigor mortis setting in,
giving way to more unpleasantness which he was instructed
to hold up as a mirror to his sexual fantasies.

He sat like a weight at one end of the see-saw
while feeling high in the air at the other,
until over time he learned how to merge

the love he felt for the radiant being he once imagined
lusting after with a love for the emptied self.
Then his fantasy no longer came to him unbidden

but moved gracefully inside his body so that
he exuded a beauty that made him seem all things
to all people when he was only being himself.

On Good and Bad

What makes the bark of a tree —
earth, sun, rain, and being what it is —
also made the flower and the apple.

What will become bark
is destined to be bark

and is perfect even though we think
it should've been a flower or an apple.

Sticks and Stones: Another Story
About the Buddha

A young man set out on a life-long journey to discover
the secret of how best to live. Collecting sticks along the way
he traded them as kindling in return for a morsel of food
and some advice on how best to live.

He collected baskets of stones, and to people's delight,
arranged them into graceful gardens of silence,
asking only for food and advice on how best to live.

Wherever he went, he traded in what wasn't wanted
for what went wanting, a stick for fire, a stone for prayer,
while the things men said about the lives they lived,
which led in all directions, allowed him to live many lives.

He learned that each man regretted the prospect of death,
and thus, regretting how he lived, lived distressed by that dilemma.
And because the paths they trod were paved with complaints
no one could see how the young Buddha lived,
by feeding sticks and stones to hunger.

Shoe Lying in a Pasture

The look in my dog's eyes seems to say
she remembers being human, the way a leather shoe
discarded in a pasture feels the place is strangely familiar.

Poor thing, continuously discharged by her senses
at the slightest movement, her liveliness is the thing
that distracts her from her life.

Meanwhile, at the other end of the leash,
her master lives like a blind man
bumping into the clutter he has made,
complaining of the things he bumps into
and not his blindness.

Seer

I was rehearsing the Sufi Three-Step
Hierarchy to the Perfection of Vision:

> to see a thing for what it is,
> then to see beneath that thing to its quality,
> then to see its eternal essence as reflected
> in every living thing,

and was about to conclude that I had attained
the Hierarchy of the Perfection of Vision
when an ugly purple bug blew against my chest
and I found myself leaping around and screaming
at a lovely, wind-blown purple blossom.

Instinct over Intellect

Fast-forwarding a video of Eavan Boland
reading her poems, she screeches to a halt
to talk about how her grandmother chased after
her grandfather's ship from port to port
to make sure he stayed faithful.

Imagine the captain spying his wife
time and time again
waving hello from the shore.

It must've been the story of how she got born.

Gain and Loss

When we fix something, at first we are happy
then we miss the moment when we fixed what annoyed us.
Then we no longer care about the comfort we brought ourselves
so much as wanting to relive the moment of bringing comfort.

It's like seeing a patch of light on the wall as part of the wall
and reasoning the light seems as solid as the wall
because of the wall, then tormenting ourselves
by thinking of the wall and light as separate
and the space we create between them
the definition of their difference.

Suhradi

An adviser to the young king explained *suhradi*,
the attitude of people who pick out a dirty spot
and then sit in it, where they feel great comfort
in criticizing others and gossiping about this one's faults
and that one's failures, in casting insults and disgracing others,
and how such a pleasure grows to become a burden until,
the adviser complained, these people make blindness an art.

The young king, in his wisdom and purity of vision, seemed
interested, and asked his learned adviser to explain it again.

Justice

That which is above is as that which is below.

• *The Tarot*

Through with ambition and too tired
for the pleasures of the body,
the old man who had willed himself
to earthly mastery desired nothing now
but to ascend to his final reward
where he would be rid of the impurities
of the life left behind.

Goodbye wife, goodbye my stalwart sons,
devoted daughters, my empire
which I cannot take with me is yours.

One last time he willed himself
to grow small, to shut down and drive headlong
into his diminishment just as a fly
on his nose tried to distract him
with its business of ablutions.

Done! Popped through, the old man had become
a globe of golden consciousness
upon which a tiny spot of gold was rotating on
what in his former life was his nose.

0

All the power that ever was or will be is here now.

• *The Pattern of the Trestleboard*

The fool is about to step off the peak
        into the empty air above the village.

The wind carries the shocked gasps
        of the people up to the fool as wind.

He seems to see something far off, the way that joy
        at merely being opens to the light.

The white sun is nearly vertical overhead. It's a minute
        before noon. It's always a minute before noon.

The little dog of the intellect looks up at his master.
        The ledge they are walking off is about to break away.

They are painted that way, incipience itself
        captured in the bright yellow sky of timelessness.

The little red feather in his cap is not big enough
        to be a wing. I find myself, unlike the fool, struggling

to not change anything, trying to not think ahead, trying
        to trust what is. This is the picture between 0 and 1.

Whatever confronts the Master,

the moment that contains him
is the moment he contains.

All things pass through him
as if he were merely passing through.

What is this perfection,
this All and Nothingness
we seek, a student asked?

The Master, sitting in the empty air
containing the world surrounding the question
containing the vision of perfection
that eluded the student,
felt moved by a great compassion
to say nothing.

Going Up, Coming Down

After fifty years of meditation, an old monk
set out to live on top of a nearby mountain
where he was determined to fast until enlightened.

On the way up, he met an old man who looked wise
and was struggling under a bundle of sticks.

"Say, old man," the monk asked, "do you know anything
about this enlightenment?" The old man, who was really
the Bodhisattva Manjusri and who was said to appear
to people when they were ready to be enlightened,
looked at the monk and in answer dropped his bundle.

The monk, in that moment, was enlightened, and said
"So that's it, that's all there is to it, just let go?"
The Bodhisattva smiled and, in answer, picked up his burden
and continued his journey.

Room

The painting, under glass, was of a desert
with a blue river running through it
which on closer inspection turned out to be a road.
What he thought was a rabbit turned out to be a rock
with cactus growing behind it. And what he mistook
for two ghosts poised to attack one another were clouds.

Something moving in the lower left-hand corner
caught his predatory eye. It was a sprig of yellow blossoms
actually waving in the wind, which on closer inspection
turned out to be his backyard reflected on the glassed-in painting.

The blank television screen reflecting him reclining in the room,
absent-mindedly staring at the painting on the wall,
trying to think of something interesting to think about,
made him realize every glass and metal object in the room
boasted a brilliant still-life on it, which, upon reflection, he thought
would be the first thing any blind man would see if he could open his eyes.

The Optimist, The Pessimist,
and The Other

The optimist believes the cup of desire
is studded with jewels
that turn out to be holes
he pours his desires through.

The pessimist, who has been through all this,
desires to pour forth his bottomless story
again and again, as if somewhere
there were a hole in it.

And the other, who seems quite ordinary,
sees the cup of desire is not out there, but within.
He says, so what if it has holes in it!

The Strongest Man in the World

My son asks in his little voice
"Will you buy me a toy?"
It's such a little voice,
such a toy voice,
that suddenly the sky flattens
like a foot coming down.

I can't resist peeling back
his voice to look behind it.
But there is only the surprise of whiteness
a Band-Aid leaves over an imagined hurt.

He thinks I am the strongest man in the world
and each evening before storytime with his mother
he asks to see my muscle.

I should buy him a toy
that asks "Will you buy me a toy?"
and then buy a smaller toy for that toy,
and so on, until the law
of diminishing returns rises up
and insults the air like disinfectant,

until I am as small and lost
as his little black firefly
lying on its back all winter
in his bug hut. Did it go on and on
about what it is to live correctly?

My son in his roomful of magical disguises,
who wants to change so much, wants
to be empowered, is telling me
when there's no voice left
beyond hearing,
there'll be no need to ask.

The Shrine

If I advertised my rug...then someone might buy it.
Then there wouldn't be an 'Arnold's Rug.'

> • GTE Yellow Pages *ad for* "Arnold's Rug Store"

In my office window there's a piece of dried out driftwood,
strung with a slack rope, that's typical of how I've rushed
to destroy in my passion to create. In this case, a bow
I made for my little son — Did I ever make the arrow? —
that, except for the idea of it, never worked.

He must've been two or three, too young to even use it,
though I remember how badly he wanted it, thrilling it
with splashes of purple paint, and then implanting
marbles all along it like cataracted eyes.

I don't know why I saved this thing just to watch it float
absently down the years with me, something torn from something
living that I modeled on the predatory wish of bringing down
something menacing and big.

I've destroyed a lot of things like that just to save them,
and I'll destroy them again, things snapped off, dried up,
cracked open, and laid to rest so they could exude their surreal
scream of loss. It's like the difference between how we live

and what we write, how we are forbidden to be sentimental
in our work though our aging faces quiver and turn royal
with nostalgia. It's the same feeling I get when I look at

what I've made, proudly displayed, and had drift back to me
again, as if loss were a shrine that kept us alive
for its own sentimental reasons, we who come to thrive
sadly and beautifully on a sense of going out of business.

One of the Small Decisions

If a man, cautious,
hides his limp,
somebody has to limp it. Things
do it; the surroundings limp.
House walls get scars,
the car breaks down; matter, in drudgery, takes it up.

• Robert Bly, "My Father's Wedding"

Because all spring my plant did badly
I wanted to cut it back to its roots.
I wanted it to fight valiantly to win itself over,
to win over itself, but it was just too weak.

I thought of pulling it out by its roots
rather than ask for advice. What I didn't want
was for the plant to grow monstrous, luminous

in my dreams, with my head on it, screaming
to the part of me that's misunderstood
and stunted, "What do you want!?"

But the great ones never go for help.
They suffer through lifetime after lifetime
to give up suffering.

Which means, as usual, I ended up doing nothing,
which for me doesn't mean nothing since it allows me
to go on and make up my mind about other things.

The Straight Line and the Water

A Zen master's life is one continuous mistake.

• the Soto Zen Master Dogen

A straight line never thinks
it's wrong. But it only shows
what it already knows.

The path that water takes
whether a trickle or a river
is always wrong, and thrives

on freedom and joy and finds
the right way mistakenly
through complete uncertainty.

Nothing can stop it
until, having tasted of
everything while remaining the same,
it ends up at its beginning.

The Wet Dog Answer

Two, three, four times a day I check on my garden
the way I used to watch my child's eyelids flickering
during sleep to see what he'd be someday.

I want my obsession to bloom
though I don't understand it,
though I've watered and pruned it
and chased the dog who was chasing away a bumblebee
sent to multiply my garden.

Is this what the old masters are doing,
those retirees who garden just before death
makes real the inner garden they can't get to,
learning to accept the not-knowing within their doing?

Like when I asked a great natural pool shark
what was his secret for staying relaxed,
and he just shook himself all over
and said, "I just go like that,"
exactly like my dog does after I spray her
for running around in mad little circles of barks
when I'm trying to correctly water my garden.

I Wish I Were a Duck

You look up the way ducks look at airplanes.

• *Alane Rollings*

I'd like to go to the park today, relax,
glide through a bouillabaisse of greenery,
watch the resident iridescent fowl sit on water,
look at the confetti of lovers and bums, the tough guys
whose eyes are still burning from scanning the want ads,
eye the lyrical girls in blazing white shorts
who seem to get off on being near trees.

A little refreshment, please.

Only they don't have gardens here in Dallas,
just scrappy little scorched brown plots with burning slides
where kids fastforward the pecking order of war.
They have a botanical garden but it costs five bucks
just to look at a table arrangement of zinnias.

I wish I were down in tropical Costa Rica, Chico,
halfway up those misty mountains where the magnificent
silver-backed gorillas would welcome me into their midst,
crooning, come on in, lie around, this is what we do all day,
groom ourselves, waiting for the big moment that never arrives.

But it's just as interesting to watch my wife
hang out the baby's torpid diapers, clouts of swaddle
dappling my line of vision like so many surrender flags.
But nowadays you've got to have a Ph.D. in thermoanesthesia
just to sit in your own backyard.

"Do you think it's gonna rain?" my wife asks.
"Not if I'm being a duck," I want to say,
but instead I bring the total immolation of half-a-century
of indecisive living down to bear on the either/or question
and say, "Yup," just so it'll give me one more inconspicuous
reason for living while I wait, prinking and preening,
forcing my mouth into a kind of wraparound might-coulda-been,
a kind of orangey handle, like a duck's.

What We Wish

• *for Jerzy and Aniela Gregorek*

When I read the poets of Poland,
who seem to have nothing
but stones and rags and the toiling
of history to sew into poems,

I feel so American, so little
of a past to have come from
I have to face the future
to figure out where I've been,

so miniscule my injustices I bemoaned
my lust for dragging off my soul
like a burdensome little sister
into some very risky business.

So all the clichés I scoffed at
were true, like The Good Old Days
I thought I was too good for when
a dose of Poland would've done me some good.

Well, now I'm not so stupid
as to curse what's left of my body
which, since the old ways are out of the question,
has become the little white flag of my wish.

Location, Location, Location

The little designer-placed apple tree on our balcony
is doubled over with the weight of its guarantee.

So the skeptic in me says this feels unreal compared to
the fire ants who've tunneled their way to light between bricks,
or the centipede who's wriggled his way to our kitchen sink
through hundreds of feet of pipe. The well-being of the tree
seems nothing compared to those struggling out of darkness.

But the improved part of me
who's trying to improve me
asks in unison with the apple tree,
"What part about being well-fed and happy is unreal?"

The Rules

My son is playing baseball.
He misses a high pop-up
and feels bad.
Then he strikes out
and we both feel bad.

But since when has paying attention
and doing well always been good for me?
I ask my dog who looks up to me
as we walk through traffic
"How many tragedies have I escaped
by not paying attention?"

My son's errors at play
are moments of pure air and light.
Isn't that what missing is?
That seems just as lovely and interesting
as getting it right.

Limits

I've filled the raft
with little puffs of breath,
just enough so I can float.

If my soul had limits
so I could blow into it
I wouldn't need the raft.

On Sitting

On the first day, the Master said to his students,
"After you have considered the chair you will sit in
as you have considered your life in relations to others —

who has more knowledge than you, who has less,
whose life is better, whose is worse;
in other words, whether it would better to be
the nail, the wood, the glue, or the varnish —
you may be seated."

Miss Stone, Miss Rose, Miss White

I am *trying* to be still
which seems contradictory
though I know the answer is buried
deep inside the time before I could speak,
thanks to those more than willing folk
who for nothing hit me on the head
when it was time for me to speak.
Be still, Mother said. How wise,

as were my illustrious elementary school teachers
who had the names of immutable objects:
Miss Stone, Miss Rose, Miss White,
my sages who, in the guise of the petty
and the inept, whose massive boredom
rammed their de-petaled love of teaching
deep into the blackout of retirement

lived like the snapshot of a still-life,
a grove of winter trees
whose skin looked like it was crawling,
whose limbs were turn-tortured by the grace
of light, whose roots were the scream of their reach
and had no idea they taught me that to surrender
one must be larger or less than one thinks.

I was a child, I didn't think. I thought
the world was mythical, engorged on promise
or stricken by neglect, I thought The Man in the Moon
was lit from within and watched the intricate figure
a waterstrider makes get erased in its going.
I looked into my teachers' eyes, past the sadness
they left on like tv stations signed off —
not there, not home, halfway in another life —
and felt them saying, "See you there"

as if they were talking to a little kid. Deeply trite,
seer-blinded, long-dead immortal Muses,
I have dedicated my life to those first words you spoke
when I was learning how to speak:
Miss Stone, Miss Rose, Miss White.

Something Important

When I mastered waiting
I loved being alone
inside the waiting
and the waiting
inside being alone.

I didn't know what I was waiting for
or why I loved being alone, just that
the deep Zen spearmint breath of timelessness
taught me how to hold back the delicious
and polish that stone with my mind
until I could accept the world
for what it was, impervious,
because I contained it.

And I wasn't anything yet.
I was a boy, water swirling
through water, which made waiting seem
like a wise decision, made me feel important,
though I looked like a battered contender
who could splatter chaos with a flight of thought.

And I still don't know what's happening,
only that when I finally go it'll all go on without me
in a form I can't imagine, and I accept that,
despite not feeling right, despite forgetting
what I'm waiting for, because there's a wisdom in me
I recognize and prize, whether or not I'm right.

Training Horses

You are alone with Alone,
and it's his move.

• *Robert Penn Warren*

Once in a while, if I lie still and am quiet,
I can still feel the trembling, prehistoric,
galactic static between stations
I used to listen to for patterns as a kid.

Marci whispered "Make friends with it,"
and blew into her stallion's nose who closed his eyes,
gathered himself, shivered, and suddenly quieted.

The stable was dark and rich and sweet and moist, and the darkness
seemed to deepen with the breathing of her exquisite horses
as she explained how her best thoroughbred was "broke to death,"
had lost his edge though he still trembled and reared and shied away
and battered his stall and roared and gnawed on wood so addictively
he would no longer stop to eat.

I couldn't read his huge brown eyes
that stretched whatever he saw across them,
but merely by the pressing of my knees or the clicking of my tongue,
I commanded his massive heart
to take the most delicate steps.

Later that night we made love and lost ourselves a bit,
and Marci slept, and I stared into the fire, bemused,
a little buzzed, my divorce about final, and listened hard
to the night that arced like a test pattern
over the little ranch and us,
but could make no sense of the quiet.

I thought it's useless to marry again and again
though nothing I knew could stop me.

Eventually, the thought of him going crazy out there
alone in the dark was enough for her to put him down.

That night I went out back to the pitch black square
where he had been kept, so I could see his stall for myself.

OneOnOne

Dante said that if you placed a mule
— by which he meant a man —
At an equal distance
Between two bales of hay
He would starve to death
In the middle of abundance

       • *Tony Hoagland*

I'm just like my aging father now,
living alone, seeing, then not seeing,
a girlfriend he always argues with
over who did what to whom,
only I don't have a girlfriend.

A cardiologist I shoot pool with,
systematic, cool, who beats me
every time, said, "You don't have a
defensive bone in your body, do you?
You'd rather have fun than win."
And though I felt flattered, I left
devastated by his wealth: Cuban cigars,
a glass house perched on a cliff in the heart
of the city, which took me forever to find.

I'd rather be me, I thought, then debated
whether to find a stunning woman in a hotspot
or just go home. I thought of the competition
at the bar, how I'd have to explain myself
like a flower, with colors and perfume and
enough see-through martinis to see me through.
But my motto is "I draw the line at emptiness," and how
if I got her home, since like me she doesn't know who
she is, we'd just accept each other for who we are,
warts, bowlegs, smashed hearts, and all.
So what's the difference, I just went home.

Somehow I believe we all come out even in the end.
I have no idea if I'm bullshitting myself unless
I'm talking about death. But on the other hand,
I have this little fire I make in my head and sit by
and drift by until, what, someone comes? No, I always
wake up when I can predict the end. On the other hand,
I tell my sons work hard, do well, because life is hard
and like the disabled athlete said, harder if you're dumb.
So either I don't believe myself or I figure I don't matter.
Probably both are true.

Now here, typically—and I could've been the genius who
put classical music to cartoons—here's where everything's supposed to
jump a plane and get bleary-eyed and lyrical,
right here so as the plane climbs there's no difference
between that little black speck and the dumbfounded blue,

like when I was a little kid and someone yelled, "Jack!"
which always sounded like a heart attack, "Look how high
that plane is!" and for all my innocent need to believe
in something transcendent, I could never see it. And if
I spotted it as it disappeared, I would have missed myself.
For me it's always been a question of not having been there.

So I could've gone to the bar and probably changed my life.
I thought about who she'd be and why she'd be there. She was sad
in my dream. I even thought of the difference between who'd be there
at 6, desperate for a date, and who'd be there at 8, just checking out
one of the many nightspots that night, and how at home, whoever she was,
she'd eventually be like me and we'd be miserable and then break up.
So the question is why do I feel the need for anyone? Why can't I live
alone and just be happy without all the trying that gets built up
like ice on the wings? Was that my original question?